A little bit of Everything

A little bit of Everything

ERYONNA NOELLE

Table of Contents

1. A Turn Down for a Turn-up — 1
2. A Choice to Love — 5
3. Don't Take it Personally — 7
4. Many to Look Back On — 9
5. Marrying the Unfinished Product — 11
6. Thankful for the Struggle — 15
7. Riding on Fumes — 19
8. Unquestionably Free! — 21
9. The Influencer — 25
10. Be a Fountain, Not a Drain — 27
11. Hearing Aid — 29
12. God as My Reference — 31
13. An Attitude of Thankfulness — 33
14. I Choose to Honor You — 35
15. Leave it to God to Provide the Mulch — 37
16. Only through Experience — 41
17. Eliminate the Distractions — 43
18. What Will You Do Today? — 45
19. Purpose Driven Decisions — 47
20. Your Happy Place — 49
21. Kill the Goliath, Spare the Saul — 51
22. The Forces that Be — 55
23. Your Greatest Enemy? YOU! — 57
24. Heart Monitor — 59
25. 4 Seasons Plus One — 61

Afterword — 65
About the Author — 69

Copyright © 2021 J Merrill Publishing, Inc.
All rights reserved. No part of this publication may be reproduced, distributed, or transmitted in any form or by any means, including photocopying, recording, or other electronic or mechanical methods, without the prior written permission of the publisher, except in the case of brief quotations embodied in critical reviews and certain other noncommercial uses permitted by copyright law. For permission requests, write to the publisher, addressed "Attention: Permissions Coordinator," at the address below.

Library of Congress Control Number: 2021924310
ISBN-13: 978-1-954414-39-6 (Paperback)
ISBN-13: 978-1-954414-38-9 (eBook)

J Merrill Publishing, Inc.
434 Hillpine Drive
Columbus, OH 43207
www.JMerrill.pub

Book Title: A Little Bit of Everything
Author: Eryonna Noelle
Cover Photography: Antonio Livingston

To my unborn promise, I hope that my life is an example that you can look at and be reminded of the grace of our Lord! So when you feel like life has had its way with you, I want you to come back to this section of the book and remember:

- Never underestimate what God has placed inside of you! You are unique!
- Like the story "Noah and the Ark," he knew nothing about building an ark. Still, through his obedience to God's instruction, he was able to complete what he was instructed to do! Not to mention he was very old, fulfilling his purpose!
- It's possible! All things are possible to them that believe! Just look in the mirror and see what was possible for me!

I love you!

A Turn Down for a Turn-up

As the year is almost complete, I find myself reflecting on many things I've gone through and how I've handled them.

One situation at my previous job ended in my resignation. I usually can find a job ASAP, but I hadn't worked for four months for some reason. During my time with God one afternoon, the Holy Spirit showed me that I'd been looking to money as my resource and not God. I was convicted, and I later repented.

Fast forward, I interviewed for two jobs. One was Monday through Friday but less pay, and the other, a financial institution that pays well, but I would have had to work on Sundays. Now, I know to some that's a no-brainer. But for me, I knew this position clashed with what God had recently instructed me to do outside of Corporate America. Normally I would have chosen the higher pay, but I didn't feel right accepting it. The word of the Lord says that "obedience is better than sacrifice."

Let me tell you this. You know you're making the right decision when you have peace or calmness surrounding that decision. But, of course, I wanted to make more money but not at the expense of winning more souls for Christ.

Needless to say, the company called me back and asked what they could do for me to accept a position with their company! Crazy huh?! I made a few small demands, including no Sundays, and got more than I asked for!

So, I encourage you, if you're in a decision-making season, even though something seems appealing, make sure the outcome lines up with God's will for your life. God knows that if I had chosen otherwise, I'd be stuck in the same cycle this time next year because the money had me comfortable.

I decided to challenge myself as I am challenging you today! Listen to the voice of the Holy Spirit. Align your will with His. Step out of your comfort zone. Things won't always be the way you planned, but when you look back, you will be able to know that THIS was nobody but God, and it could not have been better!

SCRIPTURE:

> **22** And Samuel said, Hath the Lord as great delight in burnt offerings and sacrifices, as in obeying the voice of the Lord? Behold, to obey is better than sacrifice, and to hearken than the fat of rams.

> **23** For rebellion is as the sin of witchcraft, and stubbornness is as iniquity and idolatry. Because thou hast rejected the word of the Lord, he hath also rejected thee from being king.

> **24** And Saul said unto Samuel, I have sinned: for I have transgressed the commandment of the Lord, and thy words: because I feared the people, and obeyed their voice.

— 1 SAMUEL 15:22-24

REFLECTION:

Today, send a prayer to the Father and ask for His will to become yours. Pray for a heart that embraces His desires for you rather than your own. Sometimes our desires can harm us!

A Choice to Love

Today's topic is pretty simple!

As I was scrolling through my IG (Instagram, for those that may not know, lol), I couldn't help but notice how many pictures there were of married couples. This makes my heart smile. In a world where it's praised not to have the intention to marry while dating, there are still some people who honor the sanctity of marriage.

Now, I'm not telling everyone to rush and get married, but what I am saying is that God honors marriage. So, therefore, if you desire to be wed, He will give you the desires of your heart because your heart is aligned with His!

We often walk into marriage thinking that marriage will be a bed of roses because now we're finally married, and all the hard work is behind us! Well, I'm going to be honest with you. Marriage is beautiful, but it is work! Marriage is more than a single decision, but rather one in which you choose someone over and over again, daily!

I can speak from experience. Every day you have a choice.

And the same thing is true about your relationship with God. You have a choice to read your word, pray, and live holy. It's up to you, but remember, what you choose will determine the outcome and the healthiness of your relationship with God, just as it is in a marriage.

Although my husband Shawne sometimes may make me upset, just as I'm sure I do to him, I still choose to provide wonderful home-cooked meals and do things that put a smile on his face because I love him.

I'm not saying that every day is easy for us, but I choose to speak life into our marriage by my actions. I choose to rebuke the enemy when he tries to rise up. I choose to love the gift that God has given me.

Marriage is a gift! A beautiful one!

I assure you that you will grow from being "married" to our Savior! I want to encourage you. I know that just like in a marriage, our life with God is not always easy, but you still have a choice in hard times. The choice is yours!

SCRIPTURE:

> **19** I call heaven and earth to record this day against you, that I have set before you life and death, blessing and cursing: therefore choose life, that both thou and thy seed may live:
>
> — DEUTERONOMY 30:19

REFLECTION:

> Take a moment and reflect on your commitment issues, whether to God, a spouse, or a project instructed from God. Rededicate, reassess, and refocus!

Don't Take it Personally

Let's get it right to it!! Unfortunately, some people in our lives seem to be there mainly to bring us down or see us fail. So, they may lie, cheat, backstab, or look down on you because you're not living up to their expectations of you!

But don't take it personally!

The Word of God says, in Ephesians 6:12, that we "wrestle not against flesh and blood, but against principalities, against high powers, against the rulers of the darkness of this world, against spiritual wickedness in high places."

So be strong! Yes, some things are designed to make you stumble and fall. But it's God's will that you succeed and become stronger through every test or force you encounter because He's already overcome them.

Be OK with people working against you when you've stepped up for the Kingdom! That should show you that you're making the right decision. Just know that everyone won't always agree with you or your decision. If you're facing this, don't fret. I've been where you are, and it's not easy, but it gets better day by day. The more you mature in Christ, the more you'll be able to recognize the enemy and his schemes and be able to see him coming a mile ahead!

SCRIPTURE:

10-12 And that about wraps it up. God is strong, and he wants you strong. So take everything the Master has set out for you, well-made weapons of the best materials. And put them to use so you will be able to stand up to everything the Devil throws your way. This is no weekend war that we'll walk away from and forget about in a couple of hours. This is for keeps, a life-or-death fight to the finish against the Devil and all his angels.

Ephesians 6:10-12 MSG

REFLECTION:

Take a few moments to say this prayer:

Lord, help me not to take everything so personally. Help me understand that everything is working for my good, even the things or people working against me. Give me a soft answer that turns away wrath. In your name, I pray, Amen!

Many to Look Back On

Did you ever get into something or do something that hurt at that moment, but when you look back, you die laughing?

I've had plenty of those moments because I am terribly clumsy! I can fall just standing still. It's quite funny! I can remember walking outside of the church down the steps; somehow, I ended up falling backward, landing on my back. It hurt at the moment, but I can honestly say that it's funny when I think of it now! It wasn't so bad after all. No hip replacements were needed or anything. It is just a great laugh every time I reflect on it with my family and those who were around. So many of you, like myself, have memories we can ponder. Some, we can even laugh at that probably weren't funny at the time, but we can honestly say now that it wasn't so bad!

Today, I'd like you to thank God for where you've come from, where you are now and where you're going. We now know that those situations weren't so bad because we are still standing by his grace. I'm not saying what you've been through wasn't tough or didn't hurt, but what I am saying is that the devil makes situations seem so big that all we focus on is our hurt, pain, or problem and not God. Once you realize that your current situation won't be your forever situation, you can limp on through it! It may not feel good right now, but later on, you'll be able to take joy in what you've experienced.

I can be honest with you; I've found that out for myself. I genuinely believe that having joy is a choice!

You can choose to be happy while you're going through whatever is in your path. You may feel embarrassed, hurt, or sad now, but be patient for a little while. Your most joyous days are ahead of you!

SCRIPTURE:

> **3** And not only so, but we glory in tribulations also: knowing that tribulation worketh patience;
>
> **4** And patience, experience; and experience, hope:
>
> — ROMANS 5:3-4

REFLECTION:

> Take a moment to reflect on everything you've been through up until this point. Thank God, because you are reading this devotional, you are a testament!!

Marrying the Unfinished Product

I know that if you are looking at this title, you're probably thinking, "Why in the world would anyone do that?"

Today, I just wanted to take some time to be authentic with you and help you reflect. Some time ago, while applying for jobs and watching one of my favorite shows, "Better Together," they were talking about how God loves us right where we are and married us in the state that we are in. It immediately brought another topic to mind, which is today's read.

I think about how when we're dating someone for a lengthy time, people start asking us questions like, "when do you think you'll get married?" The answer I've heard the most is, "we've got a lot of issues to work through, and I'm waiting until he or she gets "that" together before we settle down. So, we're focusing on those things right now!" That mindset prolongs the thought of marriage or makes either one or both partners hesitant because they're not yet the perfect version of the person they were looking for.

Now hear me out. I'm not saying that we shouldn't work on ourselves or become the best versions of ourselves before thinking about marriage.

But, I am saying we should look at how God took us and married us in the state we were in.

Me, I was insecure. I thought white lies were OK. I was broken but didn't want to admit it. I had a bunch of hurt from my past that I placed a Band-Aid over and was inconsistent with the blessings God had given me. I was a total mess. Yet He still chose me and chooses me still!

God saw the finished product! He knew that I'd turn out to be the amazing woman who relied on his strength to get through anything. He knew that I would help win souls to Christ one day, even through my insecurities with my voice. Unfinished, blemished, dishonest, unreliable, yet I am his!

And YOU are also His!

I love to hear my pastor say about his beautiful wife that he saw the finished product and decided to fight the odds of challenging times and choose her! That is love! To know that you're going to face some growing pains but realize that the person you are choosing is worth the sweat, the pain, and every tear.

I hope this has blessed you as much as it has blessed me. I'm rooting for you, and I want you to know that no matter what you've done, God still wants you! He'll make the most horrible part of you into a beautiful masterpiece!!

SCRIPTURE:

6-8 Christ arrives right on time to make this happen. He didn't, and doesn't, wait for us to get ready. He presented himself for this sacrificial death when we were far too weak and rebellious to do anything to get ourselves ready. And even if we hadn't been so weak, we wouldn't have known what to do anyway. We can understand someone dying for a person worth dying for, and we can understand how someone good and noble could inspire us to selfless sacrifice. But

God put his love on the line for us by offering his Son in sacrificial death while we were of no use whatever to him.

— ROMANS 5:6-8 MSG

REFLECTION:

Say this prayer with me:

> When I look in the mirror, Lord, help me see the beautiful masterpiece you've made and not just my flaws. Thank you for noticing me. I give you all of me forever and always.
>
> Amen!

Thankful for the Struggle

Now, I know you're probably thinking, "Why would anyone be thankful to struggle?" Hear me out, though!

Have you ever noticed that you only thank God for the blessings or when things are going well in your life? But, what about when things aren't so good or going so well. Are you murmuring or complaining? What about those times you've failed at a project, a marriage, a relationship, or maybe the road you traveled wasn't exactly how you expected to reach your destination, or perhaps you've even fallen short to temptation?

Listen, it's time to be thankful for the struggle too! After going through an engagement that ended terribly, I came to discover through that challenging situation where I had gone wrong and what I needed to change. My vision was clearer! In that season, I thought there was no pain greater, no greater embarrassment.

Then one day, I stopped crying over spilled milk and started thanking God for the struggle! So, I put on the garment of praise in place of the spirit of heaviness, and later I was introduced to my Boaz! (Thanks, Diamond!!) But first, I had to stop dwelling on the counterfeit.

You see, the enemy always makes it seem as though what he's got hanging over your head will keep you bound and keep you discouraged. But one thing he always forgets is Genesis 50:20 (AMP version). He meant it to harm me, but God meant it for good in order to bring about this present outcome.

If I had never experienced such a low place in my life, I would've never encountered God the way I needed in my single life. When I went to rekindle things and got rejected, I can remember bawling my eyes out in my parents' office. But, I didn't know that my rejection was God's protection! I could only see what was in front of me, but God saw what was ahead.

Joseph's life was just like that. He had no idea that his story would lead from the pit to the palace, nor could he have known how much his story would mean to so many in the future, even today. I'm sure at one point his dreams started to seem uncertain. (I am encouraged as I write this!!). Like God did with Joseph, He was letting me know, "I have something greater for you, better than the dead thing you're holding on to or what's hurting you!

All the pieces of the season you are in now are the ingredients that God is using to make you who He plans for you to be, preparing you for the place He is taking you. So, the pain, the embarrassment, and struggle turns out to be the best for us! The sweetest cake!

SCRIPTURE:

> **20** As for you, you meant evil against me, but God meant it for good in order to bring about this present outcome, that many people would be kept alive [as they are this day].
>
> — GENESIS 50:20 AMP

67 Before I was afflicted I went astray,

But now I keep *and* honor Your word [with loving obedience].

71 It is good for me that I have been afflicted,

That I may learn Your statutes.

— PSALMS 119:67,71

REFLECTION:

Today, take some time to reflect on the lowest moments of your life and begin to thank God for them. Even a bad situation can be a tool in the hand of God to produce the potential you need for Elevation!

Riding on Fumes

Have you ever been so low on gas that you knew at any moment your car would stop in the middle of the road, but at least you had to try because where you were going was so important?

I've been there too, and I believe in those moments, it was only by God's grace that we didn't end up having to push our car out of traffic. Right in time, we were able to refill.

View God's grace in this light.

Many times, many of us have been riding on fumes, and we don't even know how we've gotten anywhere lately, let alone have enough gas to make it anywhere else. Here's where God's grace steps in.

One of Webster's definitions explains that grace is: "unmerited divine assistance given to humans for their regeneration or sanctification." Or what about this one: "A state of sanctification enjoyed through divine assistance." This should let us know that we needed God's assistance to make it this far! I know many of you are riding on fumes, but I want you to know that his unmerited divine assistance is given to you! Receive it!

You may think that what you're going through is too much to handle, but Jesus tells us that his grace is sufficient for you. So, when you are weak, HIS power is being perfected through that!

Ride on grace today and always. Sometimes we don't even deserve it, but it's here for us!

SCRIPTURE:

> **9** but He has said to me, "My grace is sufficient for you [My lovingkindness and My mercy are more than enough—always available—regardless of the situation]; for [My] power is being perfected [and is completed and shows itself most effectively] in [your] weakness." Therefore, I will all the more gladly boast in my weaknesses, so that the power of Christ [may completely enfold me and] may dwell in me.
>
> — 2 CORINTHIANS 12:9 AMP

REFLECTION:

> Today, go throughout your day knowing that God loves you! I love you! Know that this season is full of grace, and His grace is there for the fullness of joy! Just in case you were wondering, YOU WILL MAKE IT!

Unquestionably Free!

One Sunday morning, before I joined the church I currently attend, I was lying in bed, and the Holy Spirit told me to forgive one of my parents. I'd been harboring unforgiveness for quite a while

Now, I don't advise you EVER to do this, but – this is me being totally transparent – I immediately said, "No! Not right now!" So, I turned over to enjoy the last five minutes of sleep (lol). And again, I heard that voice saying, "Forgive!" So, I brushed it off, got ready for church, and headed out the door. Once I arrived, my Apostle got up and said the title of his message was going to be a series on forgiveness.

I knew I had looked as though I had sucked a lemon! I couldn't believe my ears! Long story made short; he went on to speak about his testimony on forgiving his parents. Needless to say, halfway through the sermon, I was a wreck! I knew God was speaking to me! I knew that day was my time for release and freedom. The Apostle could barely get the altar call invitation out before I was one of the first to arrive. That day, I gave it all to God! Every hurt, misunderstanding, everything I couldn't understand was placed in his hands. I remember that feeling of freedom when I said, "Yes, Lord!" You can have that same feeling too!

My "yes" was simple and complete because I was saying, even if future events happen, I will still surrender to you." Later that year, I received a text from that parent asking for forgiveness. Of course, we always hear that forgiveness is not for the other person but for you. But, I am telling you, it really is! I never understood why my biological father couldn't be there for me the way I needed him to be. Still, in turn, God placed an amazing Step-Angel in my life to guide me through life!

Listen, today's focus is for those who simply need to be free; and if you feel the Holy Spirit telling you to let it go, I admonish you to be obedient. I thank God for my former Apostle, who was obedient to God in delivering that message. God used him to help me experience release. Once I was able to forgive, I was able to grow spiritually like never before.

SCRIPTURE:

36 So if the Son makes you free, then you are unquestionably free.

— JOHN 8:36 AMP

22 Samuel said,

"Has the Lord as great a delight in burnt offerings and sacrifices

As in obedience to the voice of the Lord?

Behold, to obey is better than sacrifice,

And to heed [is better] than the fat of rams.

— 1 SAMUEL 15:22 AMP

REFLECTION:

If the Son makes you free, then you are unquestionably free! Obedience is better than sacrifice, and I can say that because I've been there!

The Influencer

Have you ever been in a situation where you might have said something and immediately thought, "I probably shouldn't have said that?" Or maybe you've been in a situation that needed positive words spoken, but instead, you chose to speak death!

I honestly can't even blame you for the situations when you probably thought you could pass your remarks off with, "I was just kidding, no big deal." That's just it! We never realize how powerful our words can be. It's so simple! Whatever you speak, whether good or bad, will manifest! It's up to you to choose the outcome.

We often hear the saying, "our words have power." But what does power mean to you? I love the Oxford definition: "Power is the capacity or ability to direct or influence the behavior of others or the course of events!" What is that saying? To me, it means that our words can change the course of events. You can speak into a dead situation "come alive," and it shall. You can speak to the spirit of depression, tell it to flee, and it shall. In the name of Jesus!

SCRIPTURE:

21 Death and life are in the power of the tongue,

And those who love it *and* indulge it will eat its fruit *and* bear the consequences of their words.

— PROVERBS 18:21 AMP

REFLECTION:

The question is, do you believe what you speak? Do you believe that what you say can and will happen? Take some time today to think about your verbiage lately! Reflect and change what needs to be changed so that your words can influence whatever you may be experiencing. Remember that death and life lie in your tongue. Believe what you speak. Speak what you believe!

Be a Fountain, Not a Drain

I was driving on my way home one day and noticed a sign that said, "be a fountain, not a drain."

Immediately, that thought stood out to me and made me think, not of others, but of myself. The question was, "Am I adding value to the lives I come in contact with?"

Oftentimes we are so quick to ask the usual question, "What have you done for me?" What we should be asking, however, is, "What can I do for you? How can I serve you?"

It's our duty to serve in whatever capacity God has given us, whether at our local church, current job, or even our families. Are you willing to serve instead of being served? I genuinely believe that's what makes a great leader! We become great leaders only when we have learned to be faithful followers of Jesus Christ.

A relationship is a two-way street! You can't build anything with anyone if either of you are hardly putting something into the relationship. Are you the one constantly venting? Are you the one whose conversation is always about a bad day? Ask yourself, is your fountain healthy or poisonous? What's bleeding into your fountain that shouldn't be? We have to be careful of just wanting to be up front all the time without taking the time to pray and be a healthy lead. You can transfer unwanted spirits if you're not careful.

SCRIPTURE:

> **24** One who has unreliable friends soon comes to ruin,
>
> but there is a friend who sticks closer than a brother.
>
> — PROVERBS 18:24 NIV

> **9** Two are better than one,
>
> because they have a good return for their labor:
>
> **10** If either of them falls down,
>
> one can help the other up.
>
> But pity anyone who falls
>
> and has no one to help them up.
>
> — ECCLESIASTES 4:9-10 NIV

REFLECTION:

I challenge you to look not only at your circle of friends but look in the mirror and ask yourself, "Am I a fountain or a drain? Do I add value more than I take away? If I'm adding, what exactly am I adding?"

Be honest with yourself!

Hearing Aid

You ever heard these sayings?
You are what you eat.
Be careful what you watch!

As I've mentioned before, I thank God for the people throughout my life who've kept me accountable and pushed me to become better! One particular person is Mrs. Brown!

Mrs. Brown was like a second mom for a season in my life! I knew God placed her in my life during my twenties to help me see things a little better, dig deeper with God, and strive for success on this earth. But, one thing that she's always told me, and it stuck with me, is to "guard your ear gates."

I didn't think that much of it at that time, and I actually thought it was funny! But then, as I grew spiritually in God, her words came alive to me! I realized that to decipher the voice of God, I had to be careful to guard my hearing. I never really realized that not everything I heard wasn't good for me, that those words were sometimes even meant to harm me, or that if I let them fester and manifest, they would stunt my growth.

It is so important to watch what we are feeding into our spirits. If the old saying is true that you are what you eat, consider easily becoming what you hear. If I'm constantly surrounded by negativity, eventually, I'm going to become a person who thrives off of negativity.

But be cautious. Don't believe everything you hear, and don't immediately reject or cast down what appears to be a negative thought! Instead, test the spirit behind it to ensure it is harmful or beneficial. For example, I simply won't take advice from a bitter person, but even loving words can sting.

Our ears are more sensitive than we realize! As a result, they are easily damaged if not adequately cared for or cleaned out.

SCRIPTURE:

> **4** My dear friends, don't believe everything you hear. Carefully weigh and examine what people tell you. Not everyone who talks about God comes from God. There are a lot of lying preachers loose in the world.
>
> — 1 JOHN 4:1 MSG

REFLECTION:

> Today, take some time to clean out your ears. Any negativity (ear wax!) that's settled deep down, clean it out! Ask the Holy Spirit to tear out the roots of all negativity. Allow God's voice to become louder than any other voice or any other thing! This week focus on Spiritual music in place of R&B. Meditate on his word instead of scenario replays!

God as My Reference

In applying for a job, the company asks you for a reference for someone not related to you. Usually, they're looking for you to provide two business references and someone who can personally vouch for you!

We all know that typically, we end up putting our closest friends whom we can trust to speak well of us or that coworker we were always cool with! But, let's be honest, we've all done it once or twice! Lol!

Well, today's topic is pretty simple! Instead of using your "go-to" top three, use God as a reference for your everyday life's challenges. Understand that everything in our lives can only be obtained through God. This includes jobs, houses, cars, better financial situations, and especially spiritual freedom.

I love what it says in Acts 2: whoever calls on the Lord shall be saved. That means rescued spiritually. It's just that simple. But, just like applying for a job, it's contingent upon your references and background check. We should automatically know that, because of who God is, anything we ask for is ours! No matter how big or small, it is done! We must use him and him alone! He is the source.

SCRIPTURE:

21 And it shall come to pass, that whosoever shall call on the name of the Lord shall be saved.

— ACTS 2:21

33 But seek ye first the kingdom of God, and his righteousness; and all these things shall be added unto you.

— MATTHEW 6:33

REFLECTION:

Today, I'd like you to readjust your reference list and put God as number one! Once He is there, everything else will line up for you! Whatever you need when you call, it shall be done in Jesus' name!

An Attitude of Thankfulness

I've never been one to be a pessimist. However, not too long ago, I noticed myself complaining a lot more than I was thankful!

I would complain about cleaning up after my husband every day, all day. Then, I would complain about going to work, being in pain from endometriosis, etc.! But, like many of you, I didn't see any harm nor notice how much I did it. And then what Mrs. Brown had told me long ago finally set in.

Look at things that are going right and focus on those things, and while you're focused, you'll be so busy thanking God, you will have little time to complain! Now, I know this may seem to be hard, especially if you're not a glass-half-full type of person, but you have the power to change that!

SCRIPTURE:

16 Rejoice evermore.

17 Pray without ceasing.

18 In every thing give thanks: for this is the will of God in Christ Jesus concerning you.

— 1 THESSALONIANS 5:16-18

REFLECTION:

In a season full of opportunities to complain, thank God instead! You will notice a difference in your attitude and a brighter day! Know that you can have more joy than you've ever had, and no one can take that away!

I Choose to Honor You

Growing up, my husband and I never truly experienced what a consistent, thriving marriage looked like. By the time we had found such a couple, we had already learned bad habits and were well into our young adult years. My husband and I realized that we struggled immensely with different attributes needed to make a successful marriage because we had never seen it displayed. As a result, we found it harder to get our point across, show grace as we needed to, and continuously fill each other's love tank!

One day in prayer, the Holy Spirit convicted me, and I began to seek God to help me see my husband through his eyes. To affirm my husband instead of bringing up the bad. I have learned that this is so important as a mate. Male or female! Those around us are waiting to be affirmed, which is especially true with our spouses. And as my brother-in-law/pastor always says, "We should be the first to affirm our spouse! Nobody should beat you at doing that!"

I thank God for continuous deliverance and His grace, prompting me to have listened to the Holy Spirit! Remember, both honor and dishonor are a choice! I pray that God helps each of you quickly let go of mistakes and provide the same grace that He provides for us daily!

SCRIPTURE:

2 Set your minds on things above, not on earthly things.

— COLOSSIANS 3:2 NIV

10 Out of the same mouth come *both* blessing and cursing. These things, my brothers, should not be this way [for we have a moral obligation to speak in a manner that reflects our fear of God and profound respect for His precepts].

— JAMES 3:10 AMP

REFLECTION:

Today, focus on the good things in your spouse: strengths, beauty, tenacity, etc. Write them down if you need to! Then, release a word of affirmation once a day!

Leave it to God to Provide the Mulch

Today's topic hits home for me! Growing up, I've always been surrounded by strong women who unfortunately had their share of disappointments from people they trusted.

This affected my expectations of people. When I met someone, I assumed that I couldn't trust or open up to them no matter how nice they seemed to be. As a child, I was friendly to everybody. My dad used to say that I could talk to a dog on the street. Both Mom and Dad worried that I would get hurt should someone not be as nice in return. I was a nice, friendly child.

Even today, I still have the same heart and spirit of friendliness. Still, because of the disappointments I've had, I lost some of my ability to trust the way I should. To be honest, I'd wait for the bad in people to show up rather than giving them a complete chance at friendship! Then when delivered, I'd quickly cut them off!

Now, I'm not saying be careless with your heart, but every one of us needs to drop the "everyone-is-out-to-get-me attitude." For the people who really are out to get you, the Bible tells us in Matthew 13:24-30 that it's not your job to rip them out of your life. In due time, God will tend to them. In the meantime, He can still get the glory when we return good for evil, and by the way, He works through them to make us stronger.

He tells us that even when our enemies have planted weeds that resemble wheat in our lives, wait for the harvest season, and God will do the separating! We all know that weeds are bad for flower beds because they compete for nutrients in the soil and sunlight and cause the growth of the flowers to be stunted.

We can be assured that God is our three-layer mulch of protection around our flower beds! Even the weeds can be helpful to fertilize our soil and increase our moisture!

So yes, we are to be careful and guarded but be reminded that God can use the wheat and the weeds in the same field and still get the glory. In due time, he will do the plucking!

SCRIPTURE:

> **24** Jesus gave them another parable [to consider], saying, "The kingdom of heaven is like a man who sowed good seed in his field. **25** But while his men were sleeping, his enemy came and sowed [a]weeds [resembling wheat] among the wheat, and went away. **26** So when the plants sprouted and formed grain, the weeds appeared also. **27** The servants of the owner came to him and said, 'Sir, did you not sow good seed in your field? Then how does it have weeds in it?' **28** He replied to them, 'An enemy has done this.' The servants asked him, 'Then do you want us to go and pull them out?' **29** But he said, 'No; because as you pull out the weeds, you may uproot the wheat with them. **30** Let them grow together until the harvest; and at harvest time I will tell the reapers, "First gather the weeds and tie them in bundles to be burned; but gather the wheat into my barn."'"
>
> — MATTHEW 13:24-30 AMP

REFLECTION:

Our Savior knows what's good and bad for you. Don't be confused. God can still use what is meant to harm us to produce good in us and be glorified.

Only through Experience

In a job application, the prospective employer always provides a section to list your job qualifications as they relate to the current job you are applying for.

To think of it, I truly believe that's what our Christian walk calls for. Let's be honest. How can you counsel someone on forgiveness if you've never been in a situation where it was hard for you to forgive? How can you say God is a healer if you've never been healed from anything? Yes, we can speak prophetically, but there's something meaningful about the true and personal testament!

Don't apply for the job without the proper qualifications! Furthermore, think it not strange when you are struggling. It's building your resume! Finally, James reminds us that the testing of our faith produces endurance, leading to spiritual maturity.

Even in the natural, how do you become mature? No one is born mature. Instead, we all become mature by facing life's challenges and having the faith to endure to the end.

Our experiences are not just for our benefit. One day, those experiences will make us able to help someone else overcome. Even non-believers may discover who Christ is by our testimonies when they are going through tough days and searching for answers.

SCRIPTURE:

2 Consider it nothing but joy, my [a]brothers and sisters, whenever you fall into various trials. **3** Be assured that the testing of your faith [through experience] produces endurance [leading to spiritual maturity, and inner peace]. **4** And let endurance have its perfect result *and* do a thorough work, so that you may be perfect and completely developed [in your faith], lacking in nothing.

— JAMES 1:2-4 AMP

10 And I heard a loud voice saying in heaven, Now is come salvation, and strength, and the kingdom of our God, and the power of his Christ: for the accuser of our brethren is cast down, which accused them before our God day and night.

11 And they overcame him by the blood of the Lamb, and by the word of their testimony; and they loved not their lives unto the death.

— REVELATION 12:10-11

REFLECTION:

Today, dry your eyes! No more crying about what you're going through because now you know that it's making you stronger! Know that your testimony is going to save a life one day by leading them to Christ!

Eliminate the Distractions

When you hear the word distraction, where does your mind automatically go? Do you think Facebook? Instagram? Twitter, etc.?

For me, Facebook and TV are significant issues. It is about what the eye can see! I can look at both for hours! I'm just being honest!

I've spent much more time in the past feeding my natural eyes than my spiritual eyes! So, I want to challenge you to dig a little deeper than what the eye can see.

Start by assessing your inner circle! How often do you feel compelled by your peers to do something totally against your character? Even more sobering, what thoughts come to mind when nobody is around? The music you choose, the TV series you watch, or your books and magazines – do they feed your flesh more than your spirit?

What I'm trying to say is to consider all the factors! Reevaluate what's really taking up the majority of your time and keeping your attention when it should be on God.

The devil's desire is for us to die before we even begin to truly live!

He realizes that if he can throw you off track and get your mind off of the things of God, separating you from the divine connection with the Father and your accountability partners, he can win. You will not reach your full potential!

SCRIPTURES:

> **2** Set your affection on things above, not on things on the earth.
>
> — COLOSSIANS 3:2

> **10** The thief cometh not, but for to steal, and to kill, and to destroy: I am come that they might have life, and that they might have it more abundantly.
>
> — JOHN 10:10

REFLECTION:

> I challenge you today to ask God to place a mirror on the inside of you and reveal what truly has your heart. Then replace those things with Him! Focus on Godly things. Things that will profit you spiritually and help you succeed. Distractions are made to be defeated. Give them a "cease and desist" order and turn them over to your Defeater!

What Will You Do Today?

I saw a post on social media that stated, "I WILL finish college; I WILL be successful."

That sparked a nerve within me. It made me think, "What is God wanting to do through me today? What is His will for me this day?"

I've always been one to start something but never finish. So, let me keep it real. I've been enrolled in hair school three times. I've worked jobs and quit jobs. I've started writing and never stuck to it most of the time. But, as I've been working to better myself and serve the Kingdom of God, I have realized the Spirit of procrastination and quitting had a hold on me. So, from that point on, I demanded in Christ to be free!

Sometimes it's hard to see the end result because of distractions set before you. Maybe you don't have enough money. Perhaps you hate getting out of bed, or you have to take the bus wherever you need to go. Maybe you might have to start that company out of your living room! So be it! Like the word tells us, the race isn't given to the swift nor the battle to the strong nor bread to the wise nor riches to men of understanding nor yet favor to men of skill; but time and chance happen to them all.

Your road isn't the same as your friends or the people around you. It may take a little longer, but that's OK. You WILL finish! You WILL succeed. My church's theme for 2019 was "I can, I will, I must!" So, get an "I will" Spirit and finish strong!

SCRIPTURE:

> **11** I returned, and saw under the sun, that the race is not to the swift, nor the battle to the strong, neither yet bread to the wise, nor yet riches to men of understanding, nor yet favour to men of skill; but time and chance happeneth to them all.
>
> — ECCLESIASTES 9:11

REFLECTION:

> Allow the Holy Spirit to lead and guide you from this point on! Let go of your timeline and follow the timeline of Jesus! After all, he's a redeemer of time.

Purpose Driven Decisions

Making decisions may be easy for most, but it can sometimes be challenging for over-thinkers like myself. At times, you find yourself being indecisive.

I remember a time in my life when I was always indecisive. Later, I discovered that if I wanted my life to mean something and have purpose, I would have to change that.

Today, think about what drives you to the decisions you make. Are the decisions based on people-pleasing or living in the now? These two things are huge impactors. I appreciate my husband because, in this season, he has made us adopt the practice of not making decisions for the present but rather for the future.

To be honest, we all have made these types of decisions, even with the meals we chose. We'd rather get something instant than buy groceries to pack later in the week, even when it saves money. See how a decision so small can impact the future so much? So, the next time you find yourself in between decisions, try choosing for the future instead of the present. Every decision we make should have a purpose, a life-fulfilling purpose.

SCRIPTURE:

5 Trust in the Lord with all your heart;

do not depend on your own understanding.

6 Seek his will in all you do,

and he will show you which path to take.

— PROVERBS 3:5-6 NLT

REFLECTION:

Take some time to assess some things or situations that may cause you to be indecisive. Pray before deciding. Allow the Holy Spirit to lead you to make the right decision that will later produce purpose. Big or small!

Your Happy Place

In the hustle and bustle of everyday life, we can find ourselves a bit overwhelmed.

Some of you are moms, fathers, business owners, hard workers, dedicated friends, family! But, at the end of the day, there is never enough time in a day for you! So today, I'm challenging you to make time!

The Bible tells us to get the most out of life and have a good time. Now, don't get it twisted. Anything that doesn't align with the word of God, we know, has consequences. However, what I am saying is don't find yourself so busy with the things of life that we find no time to enjoy the things we've worked hard for and that God has blessed us with!

When was the last time you shut off your phone and took a drive? When did you really spend quality time with yourself or your spouse! When was the last time you got coffee and meditated on God's word at a beautiful park? Don't let life pass you by; trying to get by! Instead, balance and truly start to live!

SCRIPTURE:

9-13 But in the end, does it really make a difference what anyone does? I've had a good look at what God has given us to do—busywork, mostly. True, God made everything beautiful in itself and in its time—but he's left us in the dark, so we can never know what God is up to, whether he's coming or going. I've decided that there's nothing better to do than go ahead and have a good time and get the most we can out of life. That's it—eat, drink, and make the most of your job. It's God's gift.

14 I've also concluded that whatever God does, that's the way it's going to be, always. No addition, no subtraction. God's done it and that's it. That's so we'll quit asking questions and simply worship in holy fear.

15

Whatever was, is.

Whatever will be, is.

That's how it always is with God.

— ECCLESIASTES 3:9-15 MSG

REFLECTION:

If you cannot allot one hour a day for yourself or your spouse, pick one day out of the week and set that time aside for yourself!

Kill the Goliath, Spare the Saul

David was called at a young age. That didn't mean he became king overnight. And it didn't mean he would not have to go through doors that he didn't expect.

One being Saul jealous of him! Who would imagine someone you looked up to, someone you've trusted, that mentored you, being jealous of your anointing!

But, as we can see, David's eyes were so focused on the bigger picture at hand, Saul's sneaky plots could never succeed. David was focused on what he was supposed to do and who he was supposed to be.

A lot of us are focusing more on our Sauls than our calls. We are wasting our energy there when we should be preparing for Goliath! God has called us to fix our sights on bigger and greater and be conquerors. But we become distracted when we're focused on people who stand against us and attack our character. Believe me, God will avenge you, and nothing that the Goliaths or Sauls can do will harm you while you are in the will of the Lord.

SCRIPTURE:

18 When David had finished speaking to Saul, the soul of Jonathan became one with the soul of David. Jonathan loved him as himself. **2** Saul took David that day, and would not let him return to his father's house. **3** Then Jonathan made an agreement with David, because he loved him as himself. **4** Jonathan took off his long coat and gave it to David. He gave him his battle-clothes, his sword, his bow and his belt also. **5** David went everywhere that Saul sent him, and did well. Saul had him lead the men of war. And it was pleasing to all the people and to Saul's servants.

6 When David returned from killing the Philistine, the women came out of all the cities of Israel, singing and dancing, to meet King Saul, playing songs of joy on timbrels. **7** The women sang as they played, and said, "Saul has killed his thousands, and David his ten thousands." **8** Then Saul became very angry. This saying did not please him. He said, "They have given David honor for ten thousands, but for me only thousands. Now what more can he have but to be king?" **9** And Saul was jealous and did not trust David from that day on.

10 The next day a bad spirit sent from God came upon Saul with power. He acted like a crazy man in his house, while David was playing the harp. Saul had a spear in his hand, **11** and he threw the spear, thinking, "I will nail David to the wall." But David jumped out of his way twice. **12** Saul was afraid of David, because the Lord was with him but had left Saul. **13** So Saul made David go away from him, and had him lead a thousand men. And David went out to the people. **14** David did well in all that he did, because the Lord was with him. **15** When Saul saw how well he did, he was afraid of him. **16** But all Israel and Judah loved David, for he went out and came in before them.

David Marries Saul's Daughter

17 Then Saul said to David, "Here is my older daughter Merab. I will give her to you as a wife, if you only work for me with strength of heart and fight the Lord's battles." For Saul thought, "I will not go against him. Let the Philistines go against him." **18** David said to Saul, "Who am I? What is my life or my father's family in Israel, that I should be the king's son-in-law?" **19** But at the time when Saul's daughter Merab should have been given to David, she was given to Adriel the Meholathite for a wife.

20 Now Saul's daughter Michal loved David. When they told Saul, it pleased him. **21** Saul thought, "I will give her to David. I will use her to trap him, and the Philistines will go against him." So Saul said to David a second time, "Now you may be my son-in-law." **22** Then Saul told his servants, "Speak to David in secret. Tell him, 'See, the king is happy with you, and all his servants love you. So now become the king's son-in-law.'" **23** So Saul's servants said this to David. But David said, "Is it not important to you to become the king's son-in-law? I am only a poor man and am not very respected." **24** Saul's servants told Saul what David had said. **25** Then Saul said, "Say to David, 'The king wants no marriage gift except the pieces of skin from the sex parts of a hundred Philistines, to punish those who hate the king.'" Saul planned to have the Philistines kill David. **26** When his servants told this to David, it pleased him to become the king's son-in-law. Before the time was finished, **27** David and his men went and killed 200 Philistine men. Then David brought their pieces of flesh and gave all of them to the king, that he might become the king's son-in-law. So Saul gave him his daughter Michal for a wife. **28** When Saul saw and knew that the Lord was with David and that his daughter Michal loved him, **29** Saul was even more afraid of David. So he hated David always.

30 Then the Philistine leaders went out to battle. And when they did, David acted with more wisdom than all the servants of Saul. So his name became very important.

— 1 SAMUEL 18 NLV

REFLECTION:

Today, take your attention off of the Sauls in your life and put into practice some things you can do to prepare for the Goliaths!

The Forces that Be

It took me a while to realize that the problem is not the actual person behind the situation but rather the spirit using them.

For so long, some of us, like myself, cannot understand why a person is the way they are. So, we fuss and fight to get our way. But, in the end, we are left empty. This is because we're focused on the actual person instead of the spiritual forces of darkness working against us.

The agenda of the enemy is to take our focus off of the spiritual battle and trap us into fighting in the natural. However, today I am charging you to get in the spiritual fight.

Rest assured that you cannot fight a spiritual battle carnally. A spiritual fight needs no knives, no fists or bats. Instead, it requires much prayer, worship, and praise, the weapons of spiritual warfare.

Just like gravity that captures and holds objects in its power, the devil's angels attempt to do the same with us as captives to their darkness. So, stop fighting with mere words or human strategies. Instead, begin to fight on your knees where the presence of God overcomes the darkness.

SCRIPTURE:

12 For our struggle is not against flesh and blood [contending only with physical opponents], but against the rulers, against the powers, against the world forces of this [present] darkness, against the spiritual *forces* of wickedness in the heavenly (supernatural) *places*.

— EPHESIANS 6:12 AMP

REFLECTION:

This week, if you have found yourself tired of physically fighting, try fighting in prayer. Let the darkness melt like wax in the presence of God!

Your Greatest Enemy? YOU!

SO... Just in case you don't know where I am going with this, let me explain.

If you are being held back, it is not the job, not the people around you, not even the hurt you've experienced at the hands of another. It's you! You are holding yourself back!

I've realized that I'm the one who has held myself back for a long time. When it all comes down to the truth, I never believed in myself. If I had, I wouldn't have been waiting for someone else to encourage me.

We all need others who will invest in us, but first, we must invest in ourselves. We must confidently promote ourselves and be willing to work tirelessly after our 9-5 lives to write a book or open a business. We need to stop making excuses and just do it!

I had a dream some time ago, and in that dream, it was as if God was upset with me. He kept telling me over and over to just "do ministry!" I doubted the gifts, talents, dreams, and visions God has laid on my heart for years. And I know I am not the only one who has done that.

We blame others for setbacks, including our failure to believe in ourselves.

Today's reading may be a hard pill to swallow, even for myself. Still, you can only succeed and be greater once you assess honestly, accept openly, and improve purposefully!

Let go of yourself and just do the ministry! Of course, not everybody will be entirely for you all the time, but God is greater than the world against you!

SCRIPTURE:

> **13** I can do all things [which He has called me to do] through Him who strengthens *and* empowers me [to fulfill His purpose—I am self-sufficient in Christ's sufficiency; I am ready for anything and equal to anything through Him who infuses me with inner strength and confident peace.]
>
> — PHILIPPIANS 4:13 AMP

> **6** And David was greatly distressed; for the people spake of stoning him, because the soul of all the people was grieved, every man for his sons and for his daughters: but David encouraged himself in the Lord his God.
>
> — 1 SAMUEL 30:6 KJV

REFLECTION:

Today and hereafter, look at yourself in the mirror and promise yourself that you will always believe in yourself, never doubting your God-given ability! Remember, if you impact just one person, it's still an impact!

Heart Monitor

No one truly knows what's going on inside of you!

As I am writing this, we are experiencing an outbreak of the Coronavirus. As a result, it has been mandated that we all wear a mask outside of our homes. But what about the mask that we all wear every day? What are those masks covering up?

Have you ever disagreed with someone over something small, yet they got extremely irate and unwilling to resolve the issue at hand? That's because there's a deeper issue lying beneath the surface, maybe even for us.

We must be honest in every situation and get to the root of things. What caused you to really think the way you did? Why are you the way that you are? What is the what, when, where, or how behind the person you've become?

It's time to peel back the layers of that onion. Yes, the deeper we go, the more it may burn, and we may shed more tears; but it's worth it! Address what really lies beneath. It's almost like a dormant account that is still there, but nothing is coming in or going out. To make the account active again, we must deposit something that will trigger new activity in the account.

People who hurt other people have been hurt themselves and have never dealt with what was lying underneath. Their pain has been dormant, so the situation still exists. Then something is said or done that triggers the old hurt deep inside.

SCRIPTURE:

> **9-10** "The heart is hopelessly dark and deceitful,
>> a puzzle that no one can figure out.
>
> But I, God, search the heart
>> and examine the mind.
>
> I get to the heart of the human.
>> I get to the root of things.
>
> I treat them as they really are,
>> not as they pretend to be."
>
> — JEREMIAH 17:9-10 MSG

REFLECTION:

Today, ask God to perform surgery on your heart. Ask him to dig up the deep-rooted issues holding you back from trusting or believing.

4 Seasons Plus One

As I look outside my window, I see the colors of the trees changing. What was once all green is now yellow with a hint of green and orange with a touch of red. Can't you just picture it? Looking at it now, let's me know change is good! It's beautiful!

When the seasons begin to change, it is a reminder that change is inevitable and that what once was soon will not be. In just a few weeks, I'll look out and see bare trees with piles of snow.

Often, we reject change because – and let's be honest – what's unfamiliar is uncomfortable. Most change causes us to stretch, and it hurts if we're not elastic! It's not all bad, though. Many kinds of change can be for the better.

We shouldn't want to be the same person we were five years ago. It's like being married. I'm learning to discover and accept the new man my husband is becoming each day! By far, he is not the man I met, and I mean that in a good way! That glory belongs to the Lord!

Just to remind you, even though the leaves may fade, fall, and disappear, God never leaves or changes! Even through the changes in our lives, He's guiding us, shaping us, and molding us into the person He has planned, according to His will, who He wants us to be and who we long to be. So, when we pray for God to change us and make us better, most times, we have no idea what we're honestly asking for.

When we pray, we're often hoping to experience a change of season – Spring, Summer, Winter, and Fall – in our lives! But, there is another season in life, and it is the one I love most: the DUE Season! For those who believe, that is the season we should long to see.

So, welcome the changes! Welcome the leaves falling because Due season is coming, and everything due to you will be worth the struggle or the stretch!

SCRIPTURE:

> **33** He that hath received his testimony hath set to his seal that God is true.
>
> — JOHN 3:33

> **8** Jesus Christ the same yesterday, and to day, and for ever.
>
> — HEBREWS 13:8

> **11** He hath made every thing beautiful in his time: also he hath set the world in their heart, so that no man can find out the work that God maketh from the beginning to the end.
>
> — ECCLESIASTES 3:11

> **7** And he said unto them, It is not for you to know the times or the seasons, which the Father hath put in his own power.
>
> — ACTS 1:7

REFLECTION:

Thank God for the changes that have taken place in your life! The good, the bad, and the ugly! Each season was meant for the greater good for who you are and even your family, spouse, children, and friends.

Remember, although we may change and everything around us may change, God stays the same!

Afterword

A special invitation from the author:

It has been incredible sharing insights from what God has given me.

On the following pages are some topics that I hope will prompt your hearts and minds. During your time with the Father, jot down your thoughts for each one.

Here are some suggestions:

Be prayerful as you cover these topics during your time with the Father.

1. Jot down your thoughts as soon as the Holy Spirit deposits them! It happens, and it's happened to me! It's OK to come back to it later in the day!
2. Be authentic! This is something for YOU(!), and not the impressions of others.
3. Make sure it's scripturally based, back up what you've been given to write.
4. Email me at the address below once you have completed this book! Let me in on some of your notes! I love gaining new things about the Word of the Lord and seeing it in a different light! Please also let me know how this devotional has helped you in this season of your life!

eryonnabarrino@yahoo.com

DAILY TOPICS

Day 1
Attitude over Altitude

Day 2
Through the Fire but no smoke

Day 3
True Love: Is it worth the wait?

Day4
Am I my brother's Keeper?

Day5
Who I've Always wanted to be vs. Who God made me to be.

About the Author

Eryonna Barrino is a singer, songwriter, Wife, Banker (by day), and now Author of "A Little Bit Of Everything." She has traveled the world with her military roots while enjoying meeting new people and learning new cultures.

She is passionate about her ministry as a Worship Leader, Young Adult influencer, and helping people connect with Jesus Christ. Her way of Authentic Worship has helped the lives of many. Now, through this devotional, she strives to do the same.

Yonna believes that "Scars are your best teachers."

facebook.com/eryonna.barrino

www.ingramcontent.com/pod-product-compliance
Lightning Source LLC
Chambersburg PA
CBHW050740080526
44579CB00017B/98